FiESTA!

VIETNAM

GROLIER EDUCATIONAL
SHERMAN TURNPIKE, DANBURY, CONNECTICUT 06816

Published 1997 by Grolier Educational
Sherman Turnpike, Danbury, Connecticut.
Copyright © 1997 Marshall Cavendish Limited.

Set ISBN : 0-7172-9099-9
Volume ISBN : 0-7172-9115-4

Library of Congress Cataloging-in-Publication Data
Vietnam.
p.cm. -- (Fiesta!)
Includes index.
Summary: Discusses the festivals of Vietnam and how their songs, recipes, and traditions
reflect the culture of the people.
ISBN 0-7172-9115-4 (hardbound)
1. Festivals -- Vietnam -- Juvenile literature. 2. Vietnam -- Social life and customs -- Juvenile literature. [1.
Festivals -- Vietnam. 2. Holidays -- Vietnam. 3. Vietnam -- Social life and customs.]
I. Series: Fiesta! (Danbury, Conn.)
GT4878.A2V54 1997
394.269597--DC21
97-5243
CIP
AC

Marshall Cavendish Limited
Editorial staff
Editorial Director: Ellen Dupont
Series Designer: Joyce Mason
Crafts devised and created by Susan Moxley
Music arrangements by Harry Boteler
Photographs by Bruce Mackie
Subeditors: Susan Janes, Judy Fovargue
Production: Craig Chubb

For this volume
Editor: Bindu Mathur
Designer: Trevor Vertigan
Consultant: Tuyen Nguyen
Editorial Assistant: Lorien Kite

Printed in Italy

Adult supervision advised for all crafts and recipes
particularly those involving sharp instruments and heat.

CONTENTS

VIETNAM:

Vietnam is a long thin country that stretches along the coast of a peninsula in southeast Asia.

▲ **Ha Long Bay** is in the north of the country. The long coastline of Vietnam has many picturesque island caves and grottoes, as well as a number of beautiful tropical beaches.

◀ **Rice fields** are found all over Vietnam, especially around the Mekong River in the north. Rice is a staple food and is used in many different Vietnamese dishes.

China

HANOI

Hai Phong

Gulf of
Tongking

Laos

Hue

South
China Sea

Da Nang

Thailand

Mekong

Cambodia   Vietnam

Nha Trang

Hau Giang

Ho Chi Minh

Gulf of
Thailand

▲ **Buddha** is worshiped by many Vietnamese people. His image is found in many homes and temples. People also combine Buddhism with the worship of their ancestors.

▶ **City Hall** is one of the most beautiful buildings in the city of Ho Chi Minh in the south of Vietnam. The capital of Vietnam is Hanoi, which is in the north.

RELIGIONS

Vietnam has many religions that have been brought from other countries and cultures. There are also a number of native beliefs that are only found in Vietnam.

BUDDHISM is one of the most popular religions in Vietnam. One in seven Vietnamese is a Buddhist.

Buddhists believe that a young prince named Siddhartha gave up his riches to search for the meaning of life. After years of study the prince became known as Buddha, which means enlightened one.

There are more than 20,000 pagodas dedicated to Buddha in Vietnam. A pagoda is a tower with many levels and is usually found next to a temple. Buddhists go there to worship. They also practice meditation, which is a kind of praying and can be done anywhere.

Buddhist monks, or priests, wear orange or brown-colored robes and have shaved heads. They usually live in monasteries where they spend their

Village life is important to the Vietnamese people. People of many different religions and ethnic groups come together to the village market with a strong sense of community.

6

time meditating and studying the Buddhist religion. Their communities are called *sanghas*.

CATHOLICISM is the second biggest religion. There are over six million Catholics in Vietnam. The religion was brought to Vietnam by the French, Spanish, and Portuguese.

CAO DAI is the name of a religion found only in Vietnam. It is influenced mainly by Buddhism, Christianity, and Confucianism, a Chinese religion. Cao Dai has over two million followers. Another religion native to Vietnam is called Hoa Hao. Both religions come from the southern part of the country.

Vietnamese of all religions usually practice ancestor worship. They pay tribute with special rituals to family who have died. Many Vietnamese homes have an altar with pictures of their grandparents and great-grandparents.

GREETINGS FROM **VIETNAM!**

The population of Vietnam is more than 72 million. There are 54 different ethnic groups, each with a distinct language and culture. The largest group is called the Kinh. They make up almost 80 percent of the population. Other ethnic groups are the Tay, Thai, Muong, Khmer, and Nung.

Vietnamese is the language spoken by most of the population. Many Vietnamese also speak either English, French, or Chinese as a second language.

The traditional dress of Vietnam is called the *ao dai*. It is a dress with slits in the sides worn over loose-fitting pants. Both women and men wear ao dais. For women it is longer, while for men it is shorter and looser. A traditional Vietnamese hat is woven and shaped like a wide cone. It is called a *non la*.

How do you say...

Hello
Chao

Goodbye
Tam Biet

Thank you
Cam On

Peace
Binh An

ONG TAO FESTIVAL

This festival is also known as Le Tao Quan or the Kitchen God Festival. It is celebrated in December before the Vietnamese New Year. It is a time for the family to pay tribute to the Kitchen God.

The Vietnamese think that each family has a spirit that watches over them and their home. This spirit is known as the household, or kitchen, god.

During Ong Tao each home's kitchen god is replaced by a new one who will look after the family for the coming year. Before he is replaced, the old spirit rides off into the heavens and makes a report to the Jade Emperor. He informs the Jade Emperor about the family's activities for the past year. He also gives details on the state and condition of

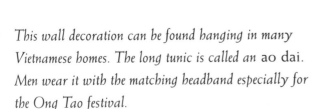

This wall decoration can be found hanging in many Vietnamese homes. The long tunic is called an ao dai. *Men wear it with the matching headband especially for the Ong Tao festival.*

Fresh carp are caught and offered to the household god for Ong Tao. The Vietnamese believe that the god rides the carp to the heavens. If he is happy, he will give a good report to the Jade Emperor.

the home. Families make a special effort to welcome the new god. They want to make sure that he will give a good report to the Jade Emperor at the end of the year.

The house is cleaned from top to bottom. Extra special attention is given to the family altar, with fresh flowers, fruit, and incense. People wear paper hats with long flaps on the sides. They also burn

gold-colored paper to honor the household god. The sounds of gongs and drums are heard in the streets as people everywhere welcome the new household god.

Ong Tao is also a time to remember family and friends who have died. The spirits of relatives and loved ones are invited back home to enjoy a meal with the living.

Each family takes extra care to make sure the household god is properly welcomed into the home. Sacrificial gold paper is burned to pay tribute to the household god.

LUNAR CALENDAR

The Ong Tao Festival takes place on the 23rd day of the last lunar month. A lunar month is different from the months used in the West. It is based on the movements of the moon. A lunar month is the time between two new moons which is around 29 days. There are 12 months in a lunar year. Buddhist festivals in Vietnam are based on the lunar calendar.

9

TET – NEW YEAR'S DAY

Also known as Tet Nguyen-Dan, this is a New Year celebration marking the first day of the lunar new year. The celebrations last for seven days. It is the largest and most colorful celebration in Vietnam.

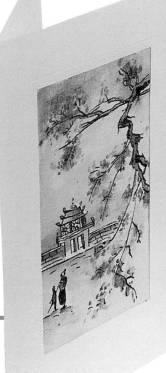

Tet is considered to be everybody's birthday. On this day everyone becomes one year older. So if a baby is born one hour before Tet, then only one hour later the child will be two years old!

Tet is traditionally a time for visiting with family and friends. It is believed that the first

GREETING CARDS

All over Vietnam people send greeting cards to friends and family for Tet. It is nice to receive a brightly colored card that says, "Chuc Mung Nam Moi," or Happy New Year! Here's how you can make your own Tet greeting card. It's so pretty, you might want to send it now!

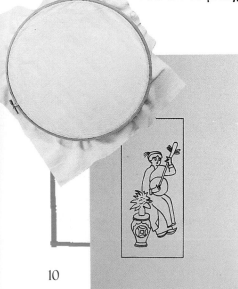

1 Stretch the cotton fabric over the hoop. Paint the fabric with white glue mixed with water and let it dry. Draw your design on white paper in black pen, marking out where the edges are. Trace the design onto the fabric in black ink, and color it in with watercolor paints.

2 Take the thin cardboard and fold into a card. Cut out the rectangular shape in the front where the painted fabric will go. Cut out your design from the fabric, and glue it onto the back of the card. Make sure it is seen clearly through the shape in the front.

visitor of the New Year to enter the house will bring either good or bad luck for the rest of the year. It is common to invite a respected person to insure good fortune for the year.

Celebrations for Tet also take place in public places. All over villages and towns in Vietnam you can see bright lights and paper decorations. Dragon and unicorn dances are also performed in the streets.

YOU WILL NEED
Thin cotton fabric
Thin white cardboard
Watercolor paints
Acrylic glue
An embroidery hoop

Dragon dances are performed by groups of dancers. If a dragon dances in front of a house, it is good luck. Children and unmarried adults receive gifts of money in red envelopes.

Nem *is a pickled pork snack that is considered to be a national delicacy of Vietnam.*
Dried fruit and vegetable candies called mut *are a common sight at Tet. They are very sweet and slightly chewy.*

Planes, trains, and buses are packed with people going home to visit family for Tet. When they get home, they can look forward to many festive foods and cakes.

In kitchens all over Vietnam people are busy cooking and preparing delicacies and special dishes for their families.

Children like to eat sweet candies called *mut* made from dried fruits and vegetables. Another special

Tet treat is called *mut hot sen*, or sweetened lotus seeds, which are small and round.

Nem is also popular for the Tet holidays. It is a pickled pork snack with sycamore leaves, and it comes wrapped up in green banana leaves. Nem is sold in bunches of five tied on a string and is a common gift for Tet.

The celebration of Tet is not complete without *banh tet* and *banh chung*. They are tasty rice cakes made with meat, beans, and vegetables wrapped and tied in banana leaves. They are then left to cook for up to ten hours.

These rice cakes are a part of many ancient legends. *Banh chung* represents the spirit of Vietnam. They are meant to be eaten in memory of distant ancestors.

Spring rolls are also prepared for Tet. They are meat and vegetables wrapped in rice pastry. Spring rolls are a popular snack throughout the year all over Vietnam.

Square-shaped rice cake banh chung *is found in the north of Vietnam. The round cake,* banh tet, *is common in the south.*

SPRING ROLLS

1 Heat 3 to 4 tbsp oil in a large skillet. Add bean sprouts, scallions, leek, carrot, and mushrooms. Stir-fry 1 minute.
2 Stir in soy sauce, sugar, and salt. Stir-fry 1 minute longer.
3 Pour vegetables into strainer in sink. Let drain 1 hour.
4 Put 2 tbsp vegetable filling on a won ton skin diagonally near a corner. Shape filling into a thin log.
5 Lift corner flap over filling, and roll once. Fold in both side corners. Roll up. Brush last corner flap with flour paste, and press to seal. Make 11 more.
6 Have an adult deep-fry spring rolls in vegetable oil at 350°F. Drain well, then eat, but be careful because filling is hot.

MAKES 12
Vegetable oil for stir-frying and deep-frying
8 oz bean sprouts, rinsed
4 scallions, minced
1 leek, finely chopped
1 carrot, grated
1½ cups sliced mushrooms
2 tbsp soy sauce
½ tsp sugar
½ tsp salt
12 large won ton skins
1 tbsp all-purpose flour mixed to a paste with 1 tbsp water

These are the five fruits of the ngu qua. *They represent the five wishes for the New Year.*

Fresh fruits are also a common sight on any Tet table. It is customary to have the *ngu qua*, or five fruits. These fruits are a banana, a tangerine, an orange, a grapefruit, and a persimmon. They represent five wishes for the New Year. People eat these fruits and hope that their wishes will come true.

People also buy kumquat trees and small orange bushes. They prune them so that they will grow

These are called mai-*apricot blossoms. They are commonly seen in the south of Vietnam. In the north they have* dao-*apricot blossoms, which are pink.*

fruit just in time for the Tet festival.

Another common decoration in front of homes is the *Cay Neu* pole. The Cay Neu is a bamboo pole that has been stripped of its leaves. A few leaves are left on top, and the pole is decorated with red paper.

There is an old legend which says that Buddha had made a deal with evil ghosts to stop bothering the people on earth. The ghosts agreed to leave and are only allowed to return to earth for Tet. But Buddha told them they had to stay away from any house with a Cay Neu pole. People put up the Cay Neu to keep their homes safe from evil spirits for Tet.

PAPER BLOSSOMS

The streets of Vietnam are filled with fragrant and colorful flowers for the Tet festival. People rush to the flower markets to buy spring blossoms to decorate their homes and to give as presents. They believe that flowers make the home more welcoming to good spirits. Other parts of the country have different-colored blossoms. You can make your own blossoms using a real tree branch and tissue paper to decorate your home or give to someone else.

YOU WILL NEED
Pink or yellow tissue paper
A leafless branch
Green-colored florist's tape
Scissors

1 Take several sheets of tissue paper, and place them on the table stacked together. Cut out the shape seen below through all the thicknesses of the tissue paper. Gather up the bottom flat edge in a bunch, and spread the tissue so it looks like a blossom. Tape the bottom in place with the green florist's tape.

1

2

2 Find a leafless branch from any tree or bush in your garden. Attach the blossoms onto the branches with the florist's tape.

HO LIM FESTIVAL

This singing festival takes place two weeks after the Vietnamese New Year. It is held in a village named Lim in the north of Vietnam.

The village of Lim comes alive with music and song during the annual Ho Lim Festival.

People train and practice singing for months in advance. They come from all over Vietnam to take part in the famous singing contest.

The competition takes place between groups of young men and women who are from different villages.

All dressed up in their finest clothes, the singers sit in groups facing each other. Then they begin to sing. The songs are about courtship and love. There are very strict rules about how the songs are sung.

The music never stops during Ho Lim. People keep singing until late in the night. Even when they leave and say goodnight, it is in the form of a song!

There are many other activities that

In the past young men and women went to the Ho Lim Festival to find their future husbands and wives. They sang a type of song called hat doi – a conversation in song.

take place during the festival. People play games like swinging and wrestling. There is a big game of chess with real people acting as the pieces. A tent is also set up for a circus.

Singers practice songs throughout the year while fishing, planting rice, or weaving hats and baskets.

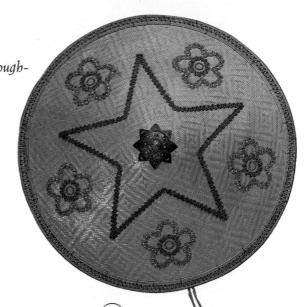

NGUOI OI!

Nguoi — oi! Nguoi o — dung ve. —— Nguoi — oi! ——
—— Nguoi o — dung ve. —— Nguoi —
ve toi va - ni —————— co
— may loi nay —————— nhoi rang — la
doi ben la —— ben song — nhu — vat — ao. Ma nay
cung co — a uot dam, ——— uot dam nhu ——
mu - a! Nguoi — oi! Nguoi o —— dung ve. ——

Please!
Stay and don't go.
As you leave,
I still have some words
to say.
Leaves change,
one side smooth,
the other rough,
like a dress.
But even they get
soaked with rain.
Please!
Stay and don't go.

PRINCESS MY CHAU OF CO LOA

The Co Loa Festival takes place near Hanoi in January. Local villagers parade in honor of King An Duong Vuong and Princess My Chau. People engage in traditional games and perform folk songs telling the story of their bravery.

THOUSANDS OF YEARS AGO Vietnam was a country called Au Lac, ruled by a great king. The king held court in the capital city of Co Loa. He had only one daughter, a beautiful princess named My Chau. She was famous for wearing a beautiful coat made of thousands of goosefeathers.

The king was very popular throughout the land. People respected him for keeping Au Lac safe from all enemies. The king was blessed by the heavens with a magic crossbow. With it he could kill thousands of enemy soldiers with just one single arrow.

No other army dared to try to invade the kingdom of Au Lac.

Knowing he could never beat the king, the general of an enemy army decided to make peace. He gave his son, Trong Thuy, to marry the king's daughter. My Chau loved her new husband very much and never wanted to be separated from him. She made a promise to scatter goosefeathers from her famous coat so he could find her if they ever lost each other.

But Trong Thuy didn't love the princess. Instead, he stole the magic crossbow to take to his father. Armed

with the magic weapon, the general attacked Au Lac. The king tried to fight back, but he was helpless without the magic crossbow. He had to escape with his daughter on horseback. He tried to hide, but the enemy was always right behind them. My Chau had kept her promise to her husband. She had scattered the goosefeathers so he could find her. This led the enemy armies right to them.

The king realized this, drew his sword, and killed his daughter. Blood from her slain body poured into the sea. Nourished by the blood of a princess, oysters at the bottom of the sea started producing precious pearls.

Her body finally washed ashore and turned into an enormous stone. Villagers built a temple next to the stone. They still come to the site to pay respects to the princess who was betrayed by her own husband.

HUNG TEMPLE FESTIVAL

On this day the Vietnamese celebrate the anniversary of the birth of their ancestors at the Hung Temple in north Vietnam.

The celebrated Hung Temple is located in the north of Vietnam. It was here that the mythical Lady Au Co gave birth to the one hundred eggs that later became the first people of Vietnam.

There are many celebrations that take place at the temple. The festivities begin on the tenth day of the third month of the lunar year, in March.

In ancient times they celebrated the festival with a unicorn dance and many games like tug of war and swinging. People made offerings of rice pies and steamed rice colored with red and violet dyes.

Today Vietnamese come from all over the country to visit the Hung Temple during the festival. They honor the memory of their ancestors and celebrate the origins of their country.

Processions made up of hundreds of people visit the many parts of the Hung

TEMPLE FESTIVALS

There are 20,000 temples in Vietnam. Most of them hold a celebration or festival once a year. In addition to paying tribute to the temple, the festival may honor some historical figure.

People observe these temple festivals by performing special rituals and ceremonies. Outside of the temple people also enjoy themselves, playing games, singing folk songs, and watching plays and dance performances. These activities are unique to each temple.

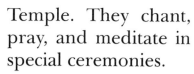

Temple. They chant, pray, and meditate in special ceremonies.

The air is filled with the smell of incense being offered by visitors. Big bronze drums and gongs can be heard everywhere.

Festivities also take place in many nearby villages. There are rowing competitions with dragon boats. People participate in games like swinging and wrestling. Special food stalls sell fresh fruit and local dishes.

The Hung Temple has a Buddhist pagoda called the Thien Quang pagoda. It is famous for its big bell tower. The temple below is called the Ngoc Son Temple. It is located near Hanoi.

LEGEND OF LAC LONG QUAN AND LADY AU CO

At the Hung Temple Festival the Vietnamese pay tribute to Lady Au Co, the Fairy Queen, and Lac Long Quan, the Dragon King. Once upon a time they gave life to a hundred sons at the Hung Temple. The Vietnamese believe these children are their ancestors.

A LONG TIME AGO before there were any people, there was a strong and fierce dragon who lived beneath the sea. He was called Lac Long Quan and ruled over the oceans. On the land lived the beautiful Lady Au Co. She was so lovely that the wind would sing songs as she walked by. She ruled over the land and was known as the Fairy Queen.

One day the mighty dragon Lac Long Quan emerged from the sea. Huge waves swirled around him as he lifted his mighty body ashore. It was then that he set eyes on the lovely Lady Au Co for the first time.

"I have never before seen such heavenly beauty," he said to the Fairy Queen. Lady Au Co was also overcome with love for the powerful beast. They were married and united their two kingdoms, the sea and the earth, in perfect harmony.

Then Lady Au Co gave birth to a hundred shiny pearl-shelled eggs. These eggs hatched into one hundred strong, healthy sons. The dragon and the Fairy Queen were overjoyed with shrimp, representing three living creatures. The *ngu qua*, or five fruits, should also be placed on the family altar. Dishes of puffed rice and boiled sweet potatoes are placed in every room for the souls of deceased family members.

Special paper is burned for Vu Lan. People believe it helps to subdue any lost or wandering souls.

But Vu Lan is not a sad time. There are many celebrations in Buddhist temples and homes. It is a time to cherish and honor the memory of those who have died.

This wooden banana tree is a decoration adorning many Vietnamese homes. It is sometimes placed on the family altar.

BAKED BANANAS

1 Heat oven to 375°F. Lightly grease a large baking dish with a little butter.

2 Put butter and sugar in a mixing bowl. Using a wooden spoon, beat until creamy.

3 Beat in cloves, orange juice, lemon juice, and ground ginger.

4 Arrange bananas in one layer in prepared dish. Spread butter mixture over bananas. Put dish in oven. Bake 10 to 15 minutes until topping is bubbling.

5 To serve, spoon bananas and juices onto plates.

MAKES 6
4 tbsp butter, at room temperature
1 cup soft brown sugar
¼ tsp ground cloves
2 tbsp orange juice
1 tsp lemon juice
¼ tsp ground ginger
6 bananas, sliced lengthwise

TET TRUNG THU

This festival is also known as the Children's or Harvest Festival. It takes place during the eighth lunar month, in late September, when the full moon is at its brightest.

Tet Trung Thu used to celebrate the beginning of the harvest. Now it is a festival for children to gather in the streets and celebrate under the full moon.

On this day you'll find the streets filled with processions of children singing to the beat of loud drums and gongs.

They also carry candles and lanterns. The lanterns come in many different shapes and sizes. There are tigers, dragons, lions, and unicorns. Today the lanterns are also made with more modern designs, such as airplanes, cars, and boats. Children all over

This child is harvesting rice in time for the Harvest Festival. The other is a follower of Buddha.

28

Vietnam receive toys and candied fruits like raisins, watermelon seeds, and sweetened lotus seeds.

Banh deo is the traditional cake for Tet Trung Thu.

An airplane lantern.

These colorful masks are worn for Tet Trung Thu.

It is made from rice flour and sugar and filled with candied fruit. Children also eat *banh trung thu*, a cake shaped like a half moon, made from egg, flour, and beans.

Lion dances are performed by groups of dancers in the streets for the Children's Festival.

THANG CUI

Cu - i   Oi!   Ta   noi   cho   cu - i   nghe.

O —— tren   cung   trang —— co —— thang   cu - i

gia   Om   mot —— moi —— mo. — Om — mot — moi — mo.

Oh Prince!
We tell you that we know,
You'd leave that palace of the moon,
To go to earth.
To go to earth.

OTHER IMPORTANT FESTIVALS

Vietnam has many different ethnic groups. They each have a unique culture and celebrate their own holidays and festivals.

BUFFALO FESTIVAL This festival is celebrated by the Bahnar people. It is held in the early spring. Buffalo are offered to thank the gods for good harvests and good health. The Bahnar also celebrate the coming of spring with javelin throwing, stick fights, and a special dance using shields.

SEC BUA FESTIVAL This is a custom of the Muong people. It takes place just before the Lunar New Year. Groups of Muong visit different homes in the village. When they arrive at the house, they sing songs for the celebration of the New Year. They play music with gongs and cymbals.

CHOM CHO NAN THO MAY FESTIVAL This is a New Year celebration of the Khmer people in the south of Vietnam. The Khmers visit the pagoda and take part in kite flying. They also put on a type of play called *du-ke*.

The skirt below is typically worn by women in the Muong ethnic group.

This is a model of a guest house of the Bahnar ethnic group. It is a place for respected visitors to stay.

WORDS TO KNOW

Altar: A table on which worshipers leave offerings, burn incense, or perform ceremonies.

Ancestor: A relation who lived a long time ago.

Ao dai: A traditional Vietnamese garment worn by both men and women. It is a dress with slits in the side worn over loose-fitting trousers.

Chanting: A type of prayer. Buddhists memorize long prayers and sing the words out loud, often with other people.

Ethnic group: A group that is held together by shared customs, language, or nationality.

Gong: A flat, round percussion instrument. It makes a long, ringing sound when hit with a hammer.

Incense: A mixture of gum and spice, often shaped into thin sticks or cones, that gives off a pleasing smell when burned.

Lunar calendar: In this calendar a month is the time between two new moons — about 29 days. Vietnamese holidays are based on this calendar.

Meditate: To sit quietly and concentrate on something, whether an idea, an object, or oneself. Meditation is an essential part of Buddhism.

Monk: A man who devotes his life to his religion and lives in a monastery.

Pagoda: A tower, usually built as part of a temple, with upward-curving roofs.

Peninsula: A strip of land surrounded on three sides by water.

Sacrifice: An offering to a god or goddess.

Temple: A place of worship. Buddhists worship in temples.

Unicorn: A mythical animal. It has the body of a horse and a single horn in the center of its forehead. The unicorn is a Buddhist symbol of wisdom.

ACKNOWLEDGMENTS

WITH THANKS TO:

Len Aldis, British-Vietnam Friendship Society. Embassy of Vietnam, London. Khong Hai, Linh Son Buddhist Temple, London. Hoa Huynh, London. Lilly Nguyen, Vietnamese Contemporary Art, London. Vale Antiques, Elgin Avenue, London hat p17.

PHOTOGRAPHS BY:

All photographs by Bruce Mackie.
Cover photograph by B. Barbey/Magnum.

ILLUSTRATIONS BY:

Fiona Saunders title page p4-5, Mountain High Maps ® Copyright © 1993 Digital Wisdom, Inc. p4-5. Tracy Rich p7. Mary van Riemsdyk p19. John Spencer p23.

SET CONTENTS